SUPER CUTE!

Baby
DUCKS

by Christina Leaf

BELLWETHER MEDIA • MINNEAPOLIS, MN

Note to Librarians, Teachers, and Parents:

Blastoff! Readers are carefully developed by literacy experts and combine standards-based content with developmentally appropriate text.

Level 1 provides the most support through repetition of high-frequency words, light text, predictable sentence patterns, and strong visual support.

Level 2 offers early readers a bit more challenge through varied simple sentences, increased text load, and less repetition of high-frequency words.

Level 3 advances early-fluent readers toward fluency through increased text and concept load, less reliance on visuals, longer sentences, and more literary language.

Level 4 builds reading stamina by providing more text per page, increased use of punctuation, greater variation in sentence patterns, and increasingly challenging vocabulary.

Level 5 encourages children to move from "learning to read" to "reading to learn" by providing even more text, varied writing styles, and less familiar topics.

Whichever book is right for your reader, Blastoff! Readers are the perfect books to build confidence and encourage a love of reading that will last a lifetime!

This edition first published in 2014 by Bellwether Media, Inc.

No part of this publication may be reproduced in whole or in part without written permission of the publisher. For information regarding permission, write to Bellwether Media, Inc., Attention: Permissions Department, 5357 Penn Avenue South, Minneapolis, MN 55419.

Library of Congress Cataloging-in-Publication Data

Leaf, Christina, author.
  Baby Ducks / by Christina Leaf.
      pages cm. – (Blastoff! Readers. Super Cute!)
  Summary: "Developed by literacy experts for students in kindergarten through grade three, this book introduces baby ducks to young readers through leveled text and related photos"– Provided by publisher.
  Audience: Ages 5-8.
  Audience: K to grade 3.
  Includes bibliographical references and index.
  ISBN 978-1-60014-973-3 (hardcover : alk. paper)
  1. Ducklings–Juvenile literature. I. Title.
  SF505.3.L43 2014
  598.4'1139–dc23
                        2013050079

Printed in the United States of America, North Mankato, MN.

Table of Contents

Ducklings!

Baby ducks are called ducklings. They have soft **down feathers**.

Ducklings **hatch** from eggs. The **brood** hatches at the same time.

Time to Swim

Mom leads her new ducklings from the nest. They **waddle** to water.

8

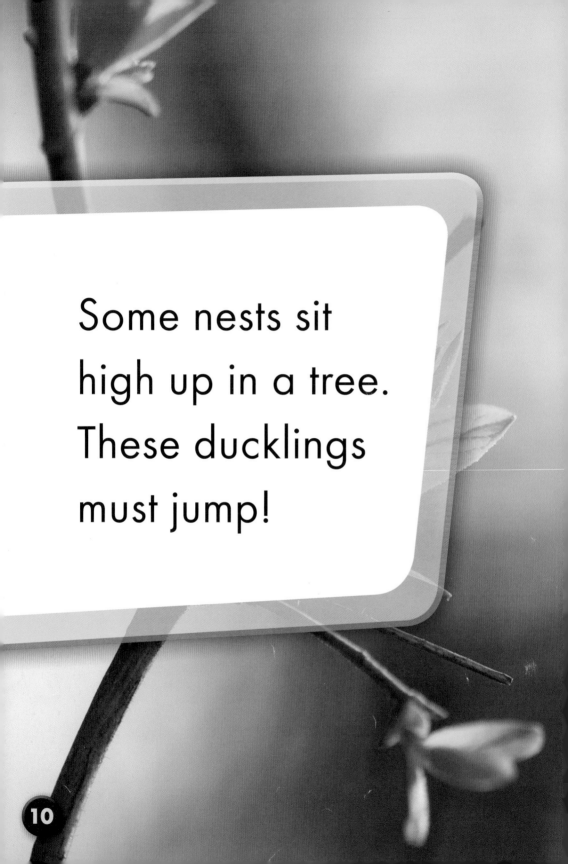

Some nests sit
high up in a tree.
These ducklings
must jump!

Ducklings float on top of the water. **Webbed feet** help them **paddle**.

webbed feet

They dip their **bills** underwater. Mom shows them which plants and **insects** to eat.

bill

Following Mom

The ducklings follow mom back to land. They swim in a line behind her.

Some ducklings catch a ride on mom's back.

Young ducklings
stick together
to stay warm.
Cuddle close!

Glossary

bills—the mouths of ducks

brood—a group of ducklings

down feathers—soft feathers that keep birds warm

hatch—to break out of an egg

insects—small animals with six legs and hard outer bodies; insect bodies are divided into three parts.

paddle—to use hands or feet to push water; ducklings paddle with webbed feet.

waddle—to move with a side-to-side motion

webbed feet—feet with thin skin that connects the toes

To Learn More

AT THE LIBRARY

Dicker, Katie. *Duck*. Mankato, Minn.: Smart Apple Media, 2014.

McCloskey, Robert. *Make Way For Ducklings*. New York, N.Y.: The Viking Press, 1941.

Zobel, Derek. *Ducks*. Minneapolis, Minn.: Bellwether Media, 2012.

ON THE WEB

Learning more about ducks is as easy as 1, 2, 3.

1. Go to www.factsurfer.com.

2. Enter "ducks" into the search box.

3. Click the "Surf" button and you will see a list of related web sites.

With factsurfer.com, finding more information is just a click away.

Index

The images in this book are reproduced through the courtesy of: sevenke, front cover; melis, pp. 4-5; imagebroker/ SuperStock, pp. 6-7, 12-13; Mikael Sundberg, pp. 8-9; Frank Greenaway/ Getty Images, pp. 10-11; Boyle & Boyle/ Agefotostock, pp. 14-15; Dennis van de Water, pp. 16-17; Stargazer, pp. 18-19; Denis Tabler, pp. 20-21.